KIND MIND CHILD

by

Mason Hughes

designed by

Hues Productions

Kind Mind Child

Text Copyright © 2024 Hues Productions
First Edition ~ May 2024

Published by HuesChild, an imprint of Hues Productions

All rights reserved.

No part of this book may be used or reproduced in any manner without written permission from the publisher except in the case of a briefly quoted review.

Author: Mason Hughes
Creative Director: B. Hughes
Executive Editor: B. Hughes
Designed by Hues Productions

Concept developed by B. Hughes of Hues Productions
Inspired by the book "Kind Mind" by Hues Productions

KINDMINDSTORE.COM

Printed in the United States of America

Library of Congress Control Number:
2024908985

ISBN:
979-8-218-41392-7

Keep good thoughts in your mind.

think it is good to be kind.

o

matter what,

know that

you're brave.

Do the best that you can do every day.

Make sure to believe that YOU can do ANYTHING!

Imagine it your own special way!

ever

give

up.

o

good.

Always.

Kindness starts with you.

Be kind with what you say.

Be kind in what you do.

There are many ways to keep a kind mind.

Just start by loving you and choosing to be kind.

KIND MIND CHILD

What could you do to keep a kind mind?

Kind Mind Child

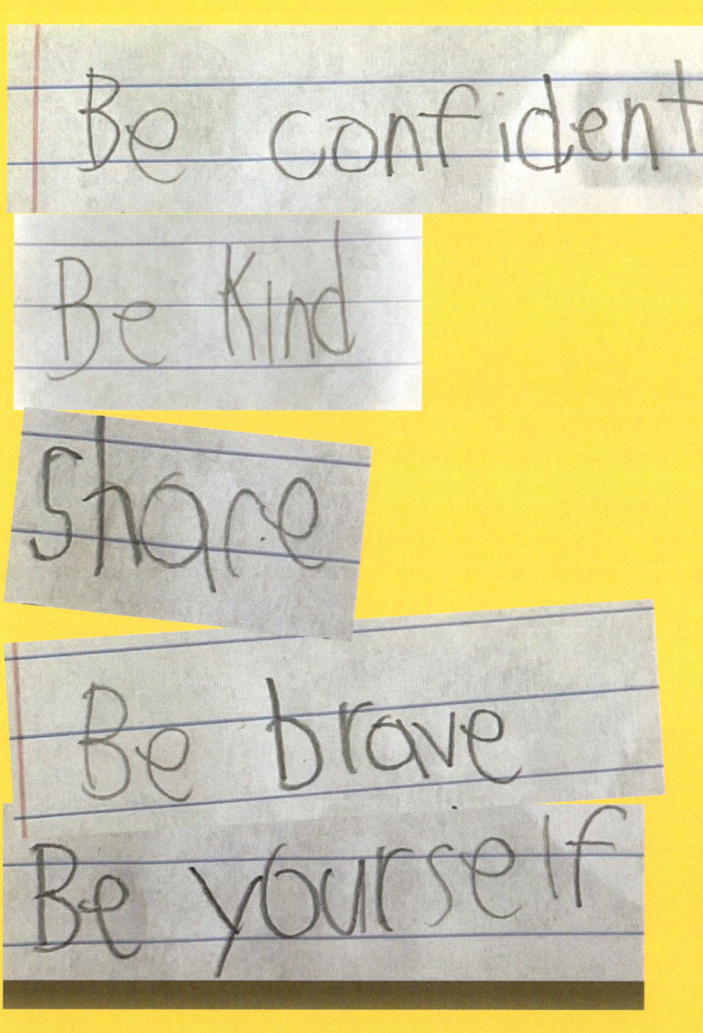

Be confident
Be kind
share
Be brave
Be yourself

THE AUTHOR
Mason Hughes

Mason created this book in collaboration with Hues Productions at age 6.

Inspired by his own experiences, Mason shares his idea of how to keep his mind kind.

www.ingramcontent.com/pod-product-compliance
Lightning Source LLC
Chambersburg PA
CBRC091203010526
44107CB00021B/1235